Prester John

FORTY SINGING SEAMEN

And Other Poems
By
ALFRED NOYES

Decorated By
E. MacKinstry

FREDERICK A. STOKES COMPANY
PUBLISHERS   NEW YORK

FORTY SINGING SEAMEN

CONTENTS

"IN OUR LANDS BE BEERES AND LYONS OF DYVERS COLOURS AS YE REDD, GRENE, BLACK, AND WHITE. AND IN OUR LAND BE ALSO UNICORNES AND THESE UNICORNES SLEE MANY LYONS. . . . ALSO THERE DARE NO MAN MAKE A LYE IN OUR LANDE, FOR IF HE DYDE HE SHOLDE INCONTYNENT BE SLEYN."—*Mediaeval Epistle, of Pope Prester John.*

To Garnett

FORTY SINGING SEAMEN

I

Across the seas of Wonderland to Mogadore we
    plodded,
  Forty singing seamen in an old black barque,
And we landed in the twilight where a Polyphemus
    nodded
  With his battered moon-eye winking red and
    yellow through the dark!
    For his eye was growing mellow,
    Rich and ripe and red and yellow,

As was time, since old Ulysses made him bellow in
    the dark!
Chorus: Since Ulysses bunged his eye up with a
    pine-torch in the dark!

II

Were they mountains in the gloaming or the giant's
    ugly shoulders
    Just beneath the rolling eyeball, with its bleared
      and vinous glow,
Red and yellow o'er the purple of the pines among
    the boulders
    And the shaggy horror brooding on the sullen
      slopes below,
      Were they pines among the boulders
      Or the hair upon his shoulders?
We were only simple seamen, so of course we
    didn't know.
Chorus: We were simple singing seamen, so of
    course we couldn't know.

III

But we crossed a plain of poppies, and we came upon
    a fountain
  Not of water, but of jewels, like a spray of
    leaping fire;
And behind it, in an emerald glade, beneath a
    golden mountain
  There stood a crystal palace, for a sailor to
    admire;
    For a troop of ghosts came round us,
    Which with leaves of bay they crowned us,
  Then with grog they well nigh drowned us, to
    the depth of our desire!
Chorus: And 'twas very friendly of them, as a
    sailor can admire!

IV

There was music all about us, we were growing
    quite forgetful
  We were only singing seamen from the dirt of
    London-town,
Though the nectar that we swallowed seemed to
    vanish half regretful
  As if we wasn't good enough to take such vittles
    down,
    When we saw a sudden figure,
    Tall and black as any nigger,
  Like the devil—only bigger—drawing near us
    with a frown!
Chorus: Like the devil—but much bigger—and he
    wore a golden crown!

V

And "What's all this?" he growls at us! With
    dignity we chaunted,

3

"Forty singing seamen, sir, as won't be put
  upon!"
"What? Englishmen?" he cries, "Well, if ye don't
  mind being haunted,
Faith you're welcome to my palace. I'm the
  famous Prester John!
    Will ye walk into my palace?
    I don't bear 'ee any malice!
One and all ye shall be welcome in the halls of
  Prester John!"
Chorus: So we walked into the palace and the halls
  of Prester John!

VI

Now the door was one great diamond and the hall
  a hollow ruby—
Big as Beachy Head, my lads, nay bigger by a
  half!

And I sees the mate wi' mouth agape, a-staring like
      a booby,
  And the skipper close behind him, with his tongue
      out like a calf!
      Now the way to take it rightly
      Was to walk along politely
Just as if you didn't notice—so I couldn't help
      but laugh!
Chorus: For they both forgot their manners and
      the crew was bound to laugh!

VII

But he took us through his palace and, my lads, as
      I'm a sinner,
  We walked into an opal like a sunset-coloured
      cloud.

5

"My dining-room," he says, and, quick as light we
    saw a dinner
  Spread before us by the fingers of a hidden fairy
    crowd;
      And the skipper, swaying gently
      After dinner, murmurs faintly,
  "I looks to-wards you, Prester John, you've done
    us very proud!"
Chorus: And we drank his health with honours,
    for he *done* us *very* proud!

VIII

Then he walks us to his garden where we sees a
    feathered demon
  Very splendid and important on a sort of spicy
    tree!
"That's the Phœnix," whispers Prester, "which all
    eddicated seamen
Knows the only one existent, and *he's* waiting for
    to flee!
      When his hundred years expire
      Then he'll set hisself a-fire
  And another from his ashes rise most beautiful
    to see!"
Chorus: With wings of rose and emerald most
    beautiful to see!

IX

Then he says, "In yonder forest there's a little silver
    river,
  And whosoever drinks of it, his youth shall never
    die!
The centuries go by, but Prester John endures
    for ever

With his music in the mountains and his magic
      on the sky!
    While *your* hearts are growing colder,
    While your world is growing older,
  There's a magic in the distance, where the sea-
      line meets the sky."
Chorus: It shall call to singing seamen till the fount
      o' song is dry!

X

So we thought we'd up and seek it, but that forest
      fair defied us.
  First a crimson leopard laughs at us most horrible
      to see,
Then a sea-green lion came and sniffed and licked
      his chops and eyed us,
  While a red and yellow unicorn was dancing
      round a tree!
    We was trying to look thinner,
    Which was hard, because our dinner
  Must ha' made us very tempting to a cat o' high
      degree!

Chorus: Must ha' made us very tempting to the
whole menarjeree!

XI

So we scuttled from that forest and across the
poppy meadows
Where the awful shaggy horror brooded o'er us
in the dark!
And we pushes out from shore again a-jumping at
our shadows,
And pulls away most joyful to the old black
barque!

And home again we plodded
While the Polyphemus nodded
With his battered moon-eye winking red and
    yellow through the dark.
Chorus: Oh, the moon above the mountains, red
    and yellow through the dark!

XII

Across the seas of Wonderland to London-town we
    blundered,
Forty singing seamen as was puzzled for to know
If the visions that we saw was caused by—here
    again we pondered—
A tipple in a vision forty thousand years ago.
    Could the grog we *dreamt* we swallowed
    Make us *dream* of all that followed?
We were only simple seamen, so of course we
    didn't know!
Chorus: We were simple singing seamen, so of
    course we could not know!

THE HIGHWAYMAN

THE HIGHWAYMAN
PART ONE

I

The wind was a torrent of darkness among the
        gusty trees,
The moon was a ghostly galleon tossed upon cloudy
        seas,
The road was a ribbon of moonlight over the purple
        moor,

And the highwayman came riding—
      Riding—riding—
The highwayman came riding, up to the old inn-
    door.

II

He'd a French cocked-hat on his forehead, a bunch
    of lace at his chin,
A coat of the claret velvet, and breeches of brown
    doe-skin.
They fitted with never a wrinkle. His boots were
    up to the thigh.
And he rode with a jewelled twinkle,
      His pistol butts a-twinkle,
His rapier hilt a-twinkle, under the jewelled sky.

III

Over the cobbles he clattered and clashed in the
    dark inn-yard.
And he tapped with his whip on the shutters, but
    all was locked and barred.
He whistled a tune to the window, and who should
    be waiting there
But the landlord's black-eyed daughter,
      Bess, the landlord's daughter,
Plaiting a dark red love-knot into her long black
    hair.

IV

And dark in the dark old inn-yard a stable-wicket
    creaked
Where Tim the ostler listened. His face was white
    and peaked.

His eyes were hollows of madness, his hair like
      mouldy hay,
But he loved the landlord's daughter,
        The landlord's red-lipped daughter,
Dumb as a dog he listened, and he heard the robber
      say —

V

"One kiss, my bonny sweetheart, I'm after a prize
      to-night,
But I shall be back with the yellow gold before the
      morning light;
Yet, if they press me sharply, and harry me through
      the day,
Then look for me by moonlight,
        Watch for me by moonlight,
I'll come to thee by moonlight, though hell should
      bar the way."

VI

He rose upright in the stirrups. He scarce could
　　reach her hand,
But she loosened her hair in the casement. His face
　　burnt like a brand
As the black cascade of perfume came tumbling
　　over his breast;
And he kissed its waves in the moonlight,
　　　　(Oh, sweet black waves in the moon-
　　　　light!)
Then he tugged at his rein in the moonlight, and
　　galloped away to the west.

PART TWO

I

He did not come in the dawning. He did not come
    at noon;
And out of the tawny sunset, before the rise of the
    moon,
When the road was a gypsy's ribbon, looping the
    purple moor,
A red-coat troop came marching—
        Marching—marching—
King George's men came marching, up to the old
    inn-door.

17

II

They said no word to the landlord. They drank his
ale instead.
But they gagged his daughter, and bound her, to
the foot of her narrow bed.
Two of them knelt at her casement, with muskets
at their side!
There was death at every window;
And hell at one dark window;
For Bess could see, through her casement, the road
that *he* would ride.

III

They had tied her up to attention, with many a
sniggering jest;
They had bound a musket beside her, with the
muzzle beneath her breast!
"Now, keep good watch!" and they kissed her.
She heard the dead man say—
Look for me by moonlight;
Watch for me by moonlight;
I'll come to thee by moonlight, though hell should
bar the way!

IV

She twisted her hands behind her; but all the knots
held good!
She writhed her hands till her fingers were wet with
sweat or blood!
They stretched and strained in the darkness, and
the hours crawled by like years,

By Moonlight

Till, now, on the stroke of midnight,
        Cold, on the stroke of midnight,
The tip of one finger touched it! The trigger at
    least was hers!

V

The tip of one finger touched it; she strove no more
    for the rest!
Up, she stood up to attention, with the muzzle
    beneath her breast.
She would not risk their hearing; she would not
    strive again;
For the road lay bare in the moonlight;
        Blank and bare in the moonlight;
And the blood of her veins, in the moonlight,
    throbbed to her love's refrain.

VI

Tlot-tlot; tlot-tlot! Had they heard it? The horse-
    hoofs ringing clear;
Tlot-tlot, tlot-tlot, in the distance? Were they deaf
    that they did not hear?
Down the ribbon of moonlight, over the brow of
    the hill,
The highwayman came riding,
        Riding, riding!
The red-coats looked to their priming! She stood
    up, straight and still.

VII

Tlot-tlot, in the frosty silence! *Tlot-tlot,* in the
    echoing night!

Nearer he came and nearer. Her face was like a
    light!
Her eyes grew wide for a moment; she drew one last
    deep breath,
Then her fingers moved in the moonlight,
       Her musket shattered the moonlight,
Shattered her breast in the moonlight and warned
    him—with her death.

VIII

He turned. He spurred to the west; he did not know
    who stood
Bowed, with her head o'er the musket, drenched
    with her own blood!
Not till the dawn he heard it, his face grew grey
    to hear
How Bess, the landlord's daughter,
       The landlord's black-eyed daughter,
Had watched for her love in the moonlight, and
    died in the darkness there.

IX

Back, he spurred like a madman, shouting a curse
    to the sky,
With the white road smoking behind him and his
    rapier brandished high.
Blood-red were his spurs in the golden noon; wine-
    red was his velvet coat;

When they shot him down on the highway,
      Down like a dog on the highway,
And he lay in his blood on the highway, with the
    bunch of lace at his throat.

  ·   ·   ·   ·   ·   ·   ·   ·   ·

X

And still of a winter's night, they say, when the
    wind is in the trees,
When the moon is a ghostly galleon tossed upon
    cloudy seas,
When the road is a ribbon of moonlight over the
    purple moor,
A highwayman comes riding—
    Riding—riding—
A highwayman comes riding, up to the old inn-door.

Over the cobbles he clatters and clangs in the dark
   inn-yard;
He taps with his whip on the shutters, but all is
   locked and barred.
He whistles a tune to the window, and who should
   be waiting there
But the landlord's black-eyed daughter,
    Bess, the landlord's daughter,
Plaiting a dark red love-knot into her long black
   hair.

BACCHUS AND THE PIRATES

BACCHUS AND THE PIRATES

Half a hundred terrible pig-tails, pirates famous in
    song and story,
  Hoisting the old black flag once more, in a palmy
    harbour of Caribbee,
"Farewell" we waved to our brown-skinned lasses,
    and chorussing out to the billows of glory,
  Billows a-glitter with rum and gold, we followed
    the sunset over the sea.

While earth goes round, let rum go round,
Our capstan song we sung:
Half a hundred broad-sheet pirates
When the world was young!

Sea-roads plated with pieces of eight that rolled to
        a heaven by rum made mellow,
Heaved and coloured our barque's black nose
        where the Lascar sang to a twinkling
        star,
And the tangled bow-sprit plunged and dipped its
        point in the west's wild red and yellow,
Till the curved white moon crept out astern like
        a naked knife from a blue cymar.

While earth goes round, let rum go round,
Our capstan song we sung:
Half a hundred terrible pirates
When the world was young!

Half a hundred tarry pig-tails, Teach, the chewer
        of glass, had taught us,
Taught us to balance the plank ye walk, your
        little plank-bridge to Kingdom Come:
Half a score had sailed with Flint, and a dozen or so
        the devil had brought us
Back from the pit where Blackbeard lay, in
        Beelzebub's bosom, a-screech for rum.

While earth goes round, let rum go round,
Our capstan song we sung:
Half a hundred piping pirates
When the world was young!

There was Captain Hook (of whom ye have heard
              —so called from his terrible cold steel
              twister,
His own right hand having gone to a shark with
              a taste for skippers on pirate-trips),
There was Silver himself, with his cruel crutch, and
              the blind man Pew, with a phiz like a
              blister,
Gouged and white and dreadfully dried in the
              reek of a thousand burning ships.

> *While earth goes round, let rum go round,*
>   *Our capstan song we sung:*
> *Half a hundred cut-throat pirates*
> *When the world was young!*

With our silver buckles and French cocked hats
              and our skirted coats (they were growing
              greener,
But green and gold look well when spliced! We'd
              trimmed 'em up wi' some fine fresh lace)
Bravely over the seas we danced to the horn-pipe
              tune of a concertina,
Cutlasses jetting beneath our skirts and cambric
              handkerchiefs all in place.

> *While earth goes round, let rum go round,*
>   *Our capstan song we sung:*
> *Half a hundred elegant pirates*
> *When the world was young!*

And our black prow grated, one golden noon, on
              the happiest isle of the Happy Islands,

An isle of Paradise, fair as a gem, on the sparkling
    breast of the wine-dark deep,
An isle of blossom and yellow sand, and enchanted
    vines on the purple highlands,
Wi' grapes like melons, nay clustering suns,
      a-sprawl over cliffs in their noonday
      sleep.

While earth goes round, let rum go round,
  Our capstan song we sung:
Half a hundred dream-struck pirates
  When the world was young!

And lo! on the soft warm edge of the sand, where
    the sea like wine in a golden noggin
Creamed, and the rainbow-bubbles clung to his
    flame-red hair, a white youth lay,
Sleeping; and now, as his drowsy grip relaxed, the
    cup that he squeezed his grog in
Slipped from his hand and its purple dregs were
    mixed with the flames and flakes of spray.

While earth goes round, let rum go round,
  Our capstan song we sung:
Half a hundred diffident pirates
  When the world was young!

And we suddenly saw (had we seen them before?
    They were coloured like sand or the pelt
    on his shoulders)

His head was pillowed on two great leopards,
 whose breathing rose and sank with his
 own;
Now a pirate is bold, but the vision was rum and
 would *call* for rum in the best of
 beholders,
And it seemed we had seen Him before, in a
 dream, with that flame-red hair and that
 vine-leaf crown.

And the earth went round, and the rum went
 round,
 And softlier now we sung:
Half a hundred awe-struck pirates
 When the world was young!

Now Timothy Hook (of whom ye have heard, with
       his talon of steel) our doughty skipper,
A man that, in youth being brought up pious,
       had many a book on his cabin-shelf,
Suddenly caught at a comrade's hand with the
       tearing claws of his cold steel flipper
And cried, "Great Thunder and Brimstone, boys,
       I've hit it at last! *'Tis Bacchus himself.*"

    And the earth went round, and the rum went
       round,
      And never a word we sung:
    Half a hundred tottering pirates
    When the world was young!

He flung his French cocked hat i' the foam (though
       its lace was the best of his wearing
       apparel):
We stared at him—Bacchus! The sea reeled
       round like a wine-vat splashing with
       purple dreams,
And the sunset-skies were dashed with blood of the
       grape as the sun like a new-staved barrel
Flooded the tumbling West with wine and
       spattered the clouds with crimson gleams.

    And the earth went round, and our heads went
       round,
      And never a word we sung:
    Half a hundred staggering pirates
    When the world was young!

Down to the ship for a fishing-net our crafty Hook
     sent Silver leaping;
Back he came on his pounding crutch, for all the
     world like a kangaroo;
And we caught the net and up to the sleeper on
     hands and knees we all went creeping,
Flung it across him and staked it down! 'Twas
     the best of our dreams and the dream
     was true.

And the earth went round, and the rum went
     round,
    And loudly now we sung:
Half a hundred jubilant pirates
When the world was young!

We had caught our god, and we got him aboard ere
        he woke (he was more than a little
        heavy);
    Glittering, beautiful, flushed he lay in the
        lurching bows of the old black barque,
As the sunset died and the white moon dawned, and
        we saw on the island a star-bright bevy
Of naked Bacchanals stealing to watch through
        the whispering vines in the purple dark!

While earth goes round, let rum go round,
   Our capstan song we sung:
Half a hundred innocent pirates
   When the world was young!

Beautiful under the sailing moon, in the tangled
        net, with the leopards beside him,
    Snared like a wild young red-lipped merman,
        wilful, petulant, flushed he lay;
While Silver and Hook in their big sea-boots and
        their boat-cloaks guarded and gleefully
        eyed him,
    Thinking what Bacchus might do for a seaman,
        like standing him drinks, as a man might
        say.

While earth goes round, let rum go round,
   We sailed away and sung:
Half a hundred fanciful pirates
   When the world was young!

All the grog that ever was heard of, gods, was it
      stowed in our sure possession?
O, the pictures that broached the skies and
      poured their colours across our dreams!
O, the thoughts that tapped the sunset, and rolled
      like a great torchlight procession
Down our throats in a glory of glories, a roaring
      splendour of golden streams!

    And the earth went round, and the stars went
      round,
     As we hauled the sheets and sung:
    Half a hundred infinite pirates
    When the world was young!

Beautiful, white, at the break of day, He woke and,
      the net in a smoke dissolving,
He rose like a flame, with his yellow-eyed pards
      and his flame-red hair like a windy dawn,
And the crew kept back, respectful like, till the
      leopards advanced with their eyes
      revolving,
Then up the rigging went Silver and Hook, and
      the rest of us followed with case-knives
      drawn.

    While earth goes round, let rum go round,
     Our cross-tree song we sung:
    Half a hundred terrified pirates
    When the world was young!

And "Take me home to my happy island!" he says.
"Not I," sings Hook, "by thunder;
We'll take you home to a happier isle, our palmy
        harbour of Caribbee!"
"You won't!" says Bacchus, and quick as a dream
        the planks of the deck just heaved
        asunder,
And a mighty Vine came straggling up that grew
        from the depths of the wine-dark sea.

And the sea went round, and the skies went
        round,
    As our cross-tree song we sung:
Half a hundred horrified pirates
    When the world was young!

We were anchored fast as an oak on land, and the
        branches clutched and the tendrils
        quickened,
And bound us writhing like snakes to the spars!
        Ay, we hacked with our knives at the
        boughs in vain,
And Bacchus laughed loud on the decks below, as
        ever the tough sprays tightened and
        thickened,
And the blazing hours went by, and we gaped
        with thirst and our ribs were racked with
        pain.

And the skies went round, and the sea swam
        round,
    And we knew not what we sung:

He rose like a flame.

37

Half a hundred lunatic pirates
When the world was young!

Bunch upon bunch of sunlike grapes, as we writhed
      and struggled and raved and strangled,
Bunch upon bunch of gold and purple daubed its
      bloom on our baked black lips.
Clustering grapes, O, bigger than pumpkins, just
      out of reach they bobbed and dangled
Over the vine-entangled sails of that most
      dumbfounded of pirate ships!

And the sun went round, and the moon came
      round,
   And mocked us where we hung:
Half a hundred maniac pirates
When the world was young!

Over the waters the white moon winked its bruised
      old eye at our bowery prison,
When suddenly we were aware of a light such as
      never a moon or a ship's lamp throws,
- And a shallop of pearl, like a Nautilus shell, came
      shimmering up as by magic arisen,
With sails of silk and a glory around it that
      turned the sea to a rippling rose.

And our heads went round, and the stars went
      round,
   At the song that cruiser sung:
Half a hundred goggle-eyed pirates
When the world was young!

Half a hundred rose-white Bacchanals hauled the
    ropes of that rosy cruiser!
Over the seas they came and laid their little white
    hands on the old black barque;
And Bacchus he ups and he steps aboard: "Hi,
    stop!" cries Hook, "you frantic old
    boozer!
Belay, below there, don't you go and leave poor
    pirates to die in the dark!"

*And the moon went round, and the stars went
    round,*
    As they all pushed off and sung:
Half a hundred riotous Bacchanals
When the world was young!

All around that rainbow-Nautilus rippled the
   bloom of a thousand roses,
Nay, but the sparkle of fairy sea-nymphs
   breasting a fairy-like sea of wine,
Swimming around it in murmuring thousands, with
   white arms tossing; till—all that *we*
   knows is
The light went out, and the night was dark, and
   the grapes had burst and their juice was
   —brine!

And the vines that bound our bodies round
  Were plain wet ropes that clung,
Squeezing the light out o' fifty pirates
  When the world was young!

. . . .

Over the seas in the pomp of dawn a king's ship
came with her proud flag flying.
Cloud upon cloud we watched her tower with
her belts and her crowded zones of sail;
And an A.B. perched in a white crow's nest, with a
brass-rimmed spy-glass quietly spying,
As we swallowed the lumps in our choking
throats and uttered our last faint feeble
hail!

And our heads went round as the ship went
round,
And we thought how coves had swung:
All for playing at broad-sheet pirates
When the world was young!

Half a hundred trembling corsairs, all cut loose,
but a trifle giddy,
We lands on their trim white decks at last and
the bo'sun he whistles us good hot grog,
And we tries to confess, but there wasn't a soul
from the Admiral's self to the gold-laced
middy
But says, "They're delirious still, poor chaps,"
and the Cap'n he enters the fact in his log,

That his boat's crew found us nearly drowned
In a barrel without a bung—
Half a hundred suffering sea-cooks
When the world was young!

Ah, yet (if ye stand me a noggin of rum) shall the
old Blue Dolphin echo the story!

We'll hoist the white cross-bones again in our palmy harbour of Caribbee!
We'll wave farewell to our brown-skinned lasses and, chorusing out to the billows of glory,
Billows a-glitter with rum and gold, we'll follow the sunset over the sea!

While earth goes round, let rum go round!
O, sing it as we sung!
Half a hundred terrible pirates
When the world was young!

E. MacKinstry
1930

THE ADMIRAL'S GHOST

THE ADMIRAL'S GHOST

I tell you a tale to-night
    Which a seaman told to me,
With eyes that gleamed in the lanthorn light
    And a voice as low as the sea.

You could almost hear the stars
    Twinkling up in the sky,
And the old wind woke and moaned in the spars,
    And the same old waves went by,

Singing the same old song
    As ages and ages ago,
While he froze my blood in that deep-sea night
    With the things that he seemed to know.

A bare foot pattered on deck;
    Ropes creaked; then—all grew still,
And he pointed his finger straight in my face
    And growled, as a sea-dog will.

"Do 'ee know who Nelson was?
    That pore little shrivelled form
With the patch on his eye and the pinned-up sleeve
    And a soul like a North Sea storm?

"Ask of the Devonshire men!
    They know, and they'll tell you true;
He wasn't the pore little chawed-up chap
    That Hardy thought he knew.

"He wasn't the man you think!
    His patch was a dern disguise!
For he knew that they'd find him out, d'you see,
    If they looked him in both his eyes.

48

"He was twice as big as he seemed;
  But his clothes were cunningly made.
He'd both of his hairy arms all right!
  The sleeve was a trick of the trade.

"You've heard of sperrits, no doubt;
  Well, there's more in the matter than that!
But he wasn't the patch and he *wasn't* the sleeve,
  And he *wasn't* the laced cocked-hat.

"*Nelson was just—A Ghost!*
  You may laugh! But the Devonshire men
They knew that he'd come when England called,
  And they know that he'll come again.

"I'll tell you the way it was
  (For none of the landsmen know),
And to tell it you right, you must go a-starn
  Two hundred years or so.

"The waves were lapping and slapping
    The same as they are to-day;
And Drake lay dying aboard his ship
    In Nombre Dios Bay.

"The scent of the foreign flowers
    Came floating all around;
'But I'd give my soul for the smell o' the pitch.'
    Says he, 'in Plymouth Sound.

" 'What shall I do,' he says,
    'When the guns begin to roar,
An' England wants me, and me not there
    To shatter 'er foes once more?'

" (You've heard what he said, maybe,
    But I'll mark you the p'ints again;
For I want you to box your compass right
    And get my story plain.)

" 'You must take my drum,' he says,
    'To the old sea-wall at home;
And if ever you strike that drum,' he says,
    'Why, strike me blind, I'll come!

" 'If England needs me, dead
    Or living, I'll rise that day!
I'll rise from the darkness under the sea
    Ten thousand miles away.'

"That's what he said; and he died;
    An' his pirates, listenin' roun',
With their crimson doublets and jewelled swords
    That flashed as the sun went down,

"They sewed him up in his shroud
    With a round-shot top and toe,
To sink him under the salt sharp sea
    Where all good seamen go.

51

"They lowered him down in the deep,
    And there in the sunset light
They boomed a broadside over his grave,
    As meanin' to say 'Good-night.'

"They sailed away in the dark
    To the dear little isle they knew;
And they hung his drum by the old sea-wall
    The same as he told them to.

.   .   .   .

"Two hundred years went by,
    And the guns began to roar,
And England was fighting hard for her life,
    As ever she fought of yore.

" 'It's only my dead that count,'
    She said, as she says to-day;
'It isn't the ships and it isn't the guns
    'Ull sweep Trafalgar's Bay.'

"D'you guess who Nelson was?
    You may laugh, but it's true as true!
There was more in that pore little chawed-up chap
    Than ever his best friend knew.

"The foe was creepin' close,
    In the dark, to our white-cliffed isle;
They were ready to leap at England's throat,
    When—O, you may smile, you may smile;

"My dead that count"

"But—ask of the Devonshire men;
   For they heard in the dead of night
The roll of a drum, and they saw *him* pass
   On a ship all shining white.

"He stretched out his dead cold face
   And he sailed in the grand old way!
The fishes had taken an eye and his arm,
   But he swept Trafalgar's Bay.

"Nelson—was Francis Drake!
  O, what matters the uniform,
Or the patch on your eye or your pinned-up sleeve,
  If your soul's like a North Sea storm?"

THE TRAMP TRANSFIGURED

THE TRAMP TRANSFIGURED

(AN EPISODE IN THE LIFE OF A CORN-FLOWER MILLIONAIRE)

I

All the way to Fairyland across the thyme and
      heather,
  Round a little bank of fern that rustled on the
      sky,
Me and stick and bundle, sir, we jogged along
      together,—
  (Changeable the weather? Well—it ain't all
      pie!)
Just about the sunset—Won't you listen to my
      story?—

Look at me! I'm only rags and tatters to your
    eye!
Sir, that blooming sunset crowned this battered
    hat with glory!
Me that was a crawling worm became a
    butterfly —
        (Ain't it hot and dry?
Thank you, sir, thank you, sir!) a blooming
    butterfly.

II

Well, it happened this way! I was lying loose and
    lazy,
    Just as, of a Sunday, you yourself might think
        no shame,
Puffing little clouds of smoke, and picking at a
    daisy,
    Dreaming of your dinner, p'raps, or wishful for
        the same:
Suddenly, around that ferny bank there slowly
    waddled—
    Slowly as the finger of a clock her shadow came—
Slowly as a tortoise down that winding path she
    toddled,
    Leaning on a crooked staff, a poor old crooked
        dame,
        Limping, but not lame,
  Tick, tack, tick, tack, a poor old crooked dame.

III

Slowly did I say, sir? Well, you've heard that funny
    fable

Consekint the tortoise and the race it give an
    'are?
This was curiouser than that! At first I wasn't able
    Quite to size the memory up that bristled thro'
        my hair:
Suddenly, I'd got it, with a nasty shivery feeling,
    While she walked and walked and yet was not a
        bit more near,—
Sir, it was the tread-mill earth beneath her feet
        a-wheeling
    Faster than her feet could trot to heaven or
        anywhere,
            Earth's revolvin' stair
    Wheeling, while my wayside clump was kind of
        anchored there.

IV

Tick, tack, tick, tack, and just a little nearer,
    Inch and 'arf an inch she went, but never gained
        a yard:
Quiet as a fox I lay; I didn't wish to scare 'er,
    Watching thro' the ferns, and thinking "What a
        rum old card!"
Both her wrinkled tortoise eyes with yellow resin
        oozing,
    Both her poor old bony hands were red and
        seamed and scarred!
Lord, I felt as if myself was in a public boozing,
    While my own old woman went about and
        scrubbed and charred!
            Lord, it seemed so hard!
    Tick, tack, tick, tack, she never gained a yard.

61

V

Yus, and there in front of her—I hadn't seen it
      rightly—
    Lurked that little finger-post to point another
      road,
Just a tiny path of poppies twisting infi-nite-ly
    Through the whispering seas of wheat, a scarlet
      thread that showed
White with ox-eye daisies here and there and chalky
      cobbles,
    Blue with waving corn-flowers; far and far away
      it glowed,
Winding into heaven, I thinks; but, Lord, the way
      she hobbles,
    Lord, she'll never reach it, for she bears too great
      a load;
        Yus, and then I knowed,
If she did, she couldn't, for the board was marked
    No Road.

VI

Tick, tack, tick, tack, I couldn't wait no longer!
    Up I gets and bows polite and pleasant as a toff—
"Arternoon," I says, "I'm glad your boots are
      going stronger;
    Only thing I'm dreading is your feet 'ull both
      come off."
Tick, tack, tick, tack, she didn't stop to answer,
    "Arternoon," she says, and sort o' chokes a little
      cough,
"I must get to Piddinghoe to-morrow if I can, sir!"

"Demme, my good woman! Haw! Don't think
    I mean to loff,"
        Says I, like a toff,
"Where d'you mean to sleep to-night? God made
    this grass for go'ff."

VII

Tick, tack, tick, tack, and smilingly she eyed me
    (Dreadful the low cunning of these creechars,
        don't you think?)
"That's all right! The weather's bright. Them
        bushes there 'ull hide me.
    Don't the gorse smell nice?" I felt my derned
        old eyelids blink!
"Supper? I've a crust of bread, a big one, and a
        bottle,"
        (Just as I expected! Ah, these creechars always
            drink!)

"Sugar and water and half a pinch of tea to rinse
  my throttle,
  Then I'll curl up cosy!"—"If you're cotched it
  means the clink!"
    —"Yus, but don't you think
  If a star should see me, God 'ull tell that star to
  wink?"

VIII

"Now, look here," I says, "I don't know what your
  blooming age is!"
  "Three-score years and five," she says, "that's
  five more years to go
Tick, tack, tick, tack, before I gets my wages!"
  "Wages all be damned," I says, "there's one thing
  that I know—
Gals that stay out late o' nights are sure to meet
  wi' sorrow.
  Speaking as a toff," I says, "it isn't *comme il faut!*
Tell me why you want to get to Piddinghoe
  to-morrow."—
  "That was where my son worked, twenty years
  ago!"—
    "Twenty years ago?
Never wrote? May still be there? Remember
  you? . . . Just so!"

IX

Yus, it was a drama; but she weren't my long-lost
  parent!
  Tick, tack, tick, tack, she trotted all the while,

64

Never getting forrarder, and not the least aware
on't,
Though I stood beside her with a sort of silly
smile
Stock-still! *Tick, tack!* This blooming world's a
bubble:
There I stood and stared at it, mile on flowery
mile,
Chasing o' the sunset.—"Gals are sure to meet wi'
trouble
Staying out o' nights," I says, once more, and
tries to smile,
"Come, that ain't your style,
Here's a shilling, mother, for to-day I've made
my pile!"

X

Yus, a dozen coppers, all my capital, it fled, sir,
Representin' twelve bokays that cost me nothink
each,
Twelve bokays o' corn-flowers blue that grew
beside my bed, sir,
That same day, at sunrise, when the sky was like
a peach:
Easy as a poet's dreams they blossomed round my
head, sir,
All I had to do was just to lift my hand and
reach:
So, upon the roaring waves I cast my blooming
bread, sir,

Bread I'd earned with nose-gays on the bare-foot
Brighton beach,
Nose-gays *and* a speech,
All about the bright blue eyes they matched on
Brighton beach.

XI

Still, you've only got to hear the bankers on the
budget,
Then you'll know the giving game is hardly
"high finance";
Which no more it wasn't for that poor old dame to
trudge it,
Tick, tack, tick, tack, on such a devil's dance:
Crumbs, it took me quite aback to see her stop so
humble,
Casting up into my face a sort of shiny glance,
Bless you, bless you, that was what I thought I
heard her mumble;
Lord, a prayer for poor old Bill, a rummy sort
of chance!
Crumbs, that shiny glance
Kinder made me king of all the sky from here to
France.

XII

Tick, tack, tick, tack, but now she toddled faster:
Soon she'd reach the little twisted by-way
through the wheat.
"Look 'ee here," I says, "young woman, don't you
court disaster!

66

Peepin' through yon poppies there's a cottage
    trim and neat
White as chalk and sweet as turf: wot price a bed
    for sorrow,
  Sprigs of lavender between the pillow and the
    sheet?"
"No," she says, "I've got to get to Piddinghoe
    to-morrow!

  P'raps they'd tell the work'us! And I've lashings
    here to eat:
      Don't the gorse smell sweet?"
Well, I turned and left her plodding on beside
    the wheat.

XIII

Every cent I'd given her like a hero in a story;
  Yet, alone with leagues of wheat I seemed to
      grow aware
Solomon himself, arrayed in all his golden glory,
  Couldn't vie with Me, the corn-flower king, the
      millionaire!
How to cash those bright blue cheques that night?
      My trouser pockets
  Jingled sudden! Six more pennies, crept from
      James knew where!
Crumbs! I hurried back with eyes just bulging
      from their sockets,
  Pushed 'em in the old dame's fist and listened for
      the prayer,
        Shamming not to care,
  Bill—the blarsted chicken-thief, the corn-flower
      millionaire.

XIV

Tick, tack, tick, tack, and faster yet she clattered!
  Ay, she'd almost gained a yard! I left her once
      again.
Feeling very warm inside and sort of 'ighly
      flattered,
  On I plodded all alone, with hay-stacks in my
      brain.
Suddenly, with *chink—chink—chink,* the old sweet
      jingle
  Startled me! *'Twas thruppence more!* Three
      coppers round and plain!

Lord, temptation struck me and I felt my gullet
tingle.
Then—I hurried back, beside them seas of golden
grain:
No; I can't explain;
There I thrust 'em in her fist, and left her once
again.

XV

Tinkle-chink! *Three ha'pence!* If the vulgar
fractions followed,
Big fleas have little fleas! It flashed upon me
there,—
Like the snakes of Pharaoh which the snakes of
Moses swallowed
All the world was playing at the tortoise and the
hare:
Half the smallest atom is—my soul was getting
tipsy—
Heaven is one big circle and the centre's
everywhere,
Yus, and that old woman was an angel and a gipsy,
Yus, and Bill, the chicken-thief, the corn-flower
millionaire,
Shamming not to care,
What was he? A seraph on the misty rainbow-
stair!

XVI

Don't you make no doubt of it! The deeper that
you look, sir,

All your ancient poets tell you just the same as
    me,—
What about old Ovid and his most indecent book,
    sir,
Morphosizing females into flower and star and
    tree?
What about old Proteus and his 'ighly curious
    'abits,
Mixing of his old grey beard into the old grey
    sea?
What about old Darwin and the hat that brought
    forth rabbits,
Mud and slime that growed into the pomp of
    Nineveh?
       What if there should be
One great Power beneath it all, one God in you
    and me?

XVII

Anyway, it seemed to me I'd struck the world's
    pump-handle!
"Back with that three ha'pence, Bill," I mutters,
    "or you're lost."
Back I hurries thro' the dusk where, shining like a
    candle,
Pale before the sunset stood that fairy finger-
    post.
Sir, she wasn't there! I'd struck the place where
    all roads crost,
All the roads in all the world. She couldn't yet
    have trotted

Even to the . . . Hist! a stealthy step behind?
      A ghost?
Swish! A flying noose had caught me round the
      neck! Garotted!
Back I staggered, clutching at the moonbeams,
      yus, almost
             Throttled! Sir, I boast
Bill is tough, but . . . when it comes to throttling
      by a ghost!

  .   .   .   .

XVIII

Winged like a butterfly, tall and slender
    Out It steps with the rope on its arm.
"Crumbs," I says, "all right! I surrender!
    When have I crossed you or done you harm?
Ef you're a sperrit," I says, "O, crikey
    Ef you're a sperrit, get hence, vamoose!"
Sweet as music, she spoke—"I'm Psyche!"—
    Choking me still with her silken noose.

XIX

Straight at the word from the ferns and blossoms
    Fretting the moon-rise over the downs,
Little blue wings and little white bosoms,
    Little white faces with golden crowns
Peeped, and the colours came twinkling round me,
    Laughed, and the turf grew purple with thyme,
Danced, and the sweet crushed scents nigh drowned
        me,
    Sang, and the hare-bells rang in chime.

71

XX

All around me, gliding and gleaming,
    Fair as a fallen sunset-sky,
Butterfly wings came drifting, dreaming,
    Clouds of the little folk clustered nigh,
Little white hands like pearls uplifted
    Cords of silk in shimmering skeins,
Cast them about me and dreamily drifted
    Winding me round with their soft warm chains.

XXI

Round and round me they dizzily floated,
    Binding me faster with every turn:
Crumbs, my pals would have grinned and gloated
    Watching me over that fringe of fern,

Bill, with his battered old hat outstanding
　　Black as a foam-swept rock to the moon,
Bill, like a rainbow of silks expanding
　　Into a beautiful big cocoon,—

XXII

Big as a cloud, though his hat still crowned him,
　　Yus, and his old boots bulged below:
Seas of colour went shimmering round him,
　　Dancing, glimmering, glancing a-glow!
Bill knew well what them elves were at, sir,—
　　Ain't you an en-to-mol-o-gist?
Well, despite of his old black hat, sir,
　　Bill was *becoming—a chrysalist*.

　　.　　.　　.　　.　　.　　.　　.　　.

XXIII

Muffled, smothered in a sea of emerald and opal,
　　Down a dazzling gulf of dreams I sank and sank
　　　　away,
Wound about with twenty thousand yards of silken
　　　　rope, all
　　Shimmering into crimson, glimmering into grey,
Drowsing, waking, living, dying, just as you
　　　　　regards it,
　　Buried in a sunset-cloud, or cloud of breaking
　　　　day,
'Cording as from East or West yourself might look
　　　　towards it,
　　Losing, gaining, lost in darkness, ragged, grimy,
　　　　gay,
　　　　　'And-cuffed, not to say
　　Gagged, but both my shoulders budding,
　　　　　sprouting white as May.

73

XXIV

Sprouting like the milky buds o' hawthorn in the
    night-time,
Pouting like the snowy buds o' roses in July,
Spreading in my chrysalist and waiting for the right
    time,
    When—I thought—they'd bust to wings and Bill
    would rise and fly,
Tick, tack, tick, tack, as if it came in answer,
    Sweeping o'er my head again the tide o' dreams
    went by,—
I must get to Piddinghoe to-morrow if I can, sir,
    Tick, tack, a crackle in my chrysalist, a cry!
        Then the warm blue sky
    Bust the shell, and out crept Bill—a blooming
    butterfly!

   •   •   •   •   •   •   •   •   •

XXV

Blue as a corn-flower, blazed the zenith: the
      deepening East like a scarlet poppy
Burned while, dazzled with golden bloom, white
      clouds like daisies, green seas like wheat,
Gripping the sign-post, first, I climbs, to sun my
      wings, which were wrinkled and floppy,
Spreading 'em white o'er the words *No Road*, and
      hanging fast by my six black feet.

XXVI

Still on my head was the battered old beaver, but
      through it my clubbed antennae slanted,
("Feelers" yourself would probably call 'em) my
      battered old boots were hardly seen
Under the golden fluff of the tail! It was Bill, sir,
      Bill, though highly enchanted,
Spreading his beautiful snow-white pinions,
      tipped with orange, and veined with
      green.

XXVII

Yus, old Bill was an Orange-tip, a spirit in glory,
      a blooming Psyche!
New, it was new from East to West this rummy
      old world that I dreamed I knew,
How can I tell you the things that I saw with my—
      what shall *I* call 'em? — "feelers?" — O,
      crikey,
"Feelers?" You know how the man born blind
      described such colours as scarlet or blue.

XXVIII

"Scarlet," he says, "is the sound of a trumpet, blue
    is a flute," for he hasn't a notion!
No, nor nobody living on earth can tell it him
    plain, if he hasn't the sight!
That's how it stands with ragged old Bill, a-drift
    and a-dream on a measureless ocean,
Gifted wi' fifteen new-born senses, and seeing you
    blind to their new strange light.

XXIX

How can I tell you? Sir, you must wait, till you die
    like Bill, ere you understand it!
Only—I saw—the same as a bee that strikes to
    his hive ten leagues away—
Straight as a die, while I winked and blinked on
    that sun-warmed wood and my wings
    expanded
(Whistler drawings that men call wings)—I saw
    —and I flew—that's all I can say.

XXX

Flew over leagues of whispering wonder, fairy
      forests and flowery palaces,
  Love-lorn casements, delicate kingdoms,
      beautiful flaming thoughts of—Him;
Feasts of a million blue-mailed angels lifting their
      honey-and-wine-brimmed chalices,
  Throned upon clouds—(which you'd call white
      clover) down to the world's most rosiest
      rim.

XXXI

New and new and new and new, the white o' the
      cliffs and the wind in the heather,
  Yus, and the sea-gulls flying like flakes of the sea
      that flashed to the new-born day,
Song, song, song, song, quivering up in the wild
      blue weather,
  Thousands of seraphim singing together, and me
      just flying and—*knowing my way*.

XXXII

Straight as a die to Piddinghoe's dolphin, and there
      I drops in a cottage garden,
  There, on a sun-warmed window-sill, I winks
      and peeps, for the window was wide!
Crumbs, he was there and fast in her arms and
      a-begging his poor old mother's pardon,
  There with his lips on her old grey hair, and her
      head on his breast while she laughed and
      cried,—

XXXIII

"One and nine-pence that old tramp gave me, or else
    I should never have reached you, sonny,
Never, and you just leaving the village to-day
    and meaning to cross the sea,
One and nine-pence he gave me, I paid for the
    farmer's lift with half o' the money!
Here's the ten-pence halfpenny, sonny, 'twill pay
    for our little 'ouse-warming tea."

   .   .   .   .

XXXIV

Tick, tack, tick, tack, out into the garden
   Toddles that old Fairy with his arm about her
       —so,
Cuddling of her still, and still a-begging of her
       pardon,
   While she says "I wish the corn-flower king could
       only know!
Bless him, bless him, once again," she says and softly
       gazes
   Up to heaven, a-smiling in her mutch as white
       as snow,
All among her gilly-flowers and stocks and double
       daisies,
   Mignonette, forget-me-not, . . . *Twenty years
       ago,*
       All a rosy glow,
This is how it was, she said, *twenty years ago.*

   .   .   .   .

XXXV

Once again I seemed to wake, the vision it had fled,
       sir,
   There I lay upon the downs: the sky was like a
       peach;
Yus, with twelve bokays of corn-flowers blue beside
       my bed, sir,
   More than usual 'andsome, so they'd bring me
       two-pence each.
Easy as a poet's dreams they blossomed round my
       head, sir,

All I had to do was just to lift my hand and reach,
Tie 'em with a bit of string, and earn my blooming
bread, sir,
Selling little nose-gays on the bare-foot Brighton
beach,
Nose-gays *and* a speech,
All about the bright blue eyes they matched on
Brighton beach.

XXXVI

Overhead the singing lark and underfoot the
heather,
Far and blue in front of us the unplumbed sky,
Me and stick and bundle, O, we jogs along together,
(Changeable the weather? Well, it ain't all pie!)
Weather's like a woman, sir, and if she wants to
quarrel,
If her eyes begin to flash and hair begins to fly,
You've to wait a little, then—the story has a
moral—
Ain't the sunny kisses all the sweeter bye and
bye?—
(Crumbs, it's 'ot and dry!
Thank you, sir! Thank you, sir!) the sweeter
bye and bye.

XXXVII

So the world's my sweetheart and I sort of want to
squeeze 'er.
Toffs 'ull get no chance of heaven, take 'em in
the lump!

So the world's my sweetheart

81

Never laid in hay-fields when the dawn came over-
  sea, sir?
  Guess it's true that story 'bout the needle and
    the hump!
Never crept into a stack because the wind was
    blowing,
  Hollered out a nest and closed the door-way with
    a clump,
Laid and heard the whisper of the silence, growing,
    growing,
  Watched a thousand wheeling stars and
    wondered if they'd bump?
      What I say would stump
  Joshua! But I've done it, sir. Don't think I'm
    off my chump.

XXXVIII

If you try and lay, sir, with your face turned up to
    wonder,
  Up to twenty million miles of stars that roll like
    one,
Right across to God knows where, and you just
    huddled under
  Like a little beetle with no business of his own,
There you'd hear — like growing grass — a funny
    silent sound, sir,
  Mixed with curious crackles in a steady
    undertone,
Just the sound of twenty billion stars a-going
    round, sir,

Yus, and you beneath 'em like a wise old ant,
   alone,
       Ant upon a stone,
Waving of his antlers, on the Sussex downs,
   alone.

TALES OF THE
MERMAID TAVERN

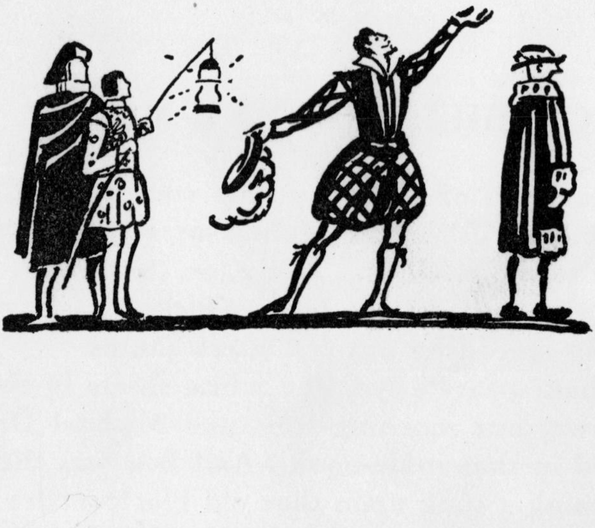

BLACK BILL'S HONEY-MOON

The garlands of a Whitsun ale were strewn
About our rushes, the night that Raleigh brought
Bacon to sup with us. There, on that night,
I saw the singer of the *Faerie Queen*
Quietly spreading out his latest cantos
For Shakespeare's eye, like white sheets in the sun.
Marlowe, our morning-star, and Michael Drayton
Talked in that ingle-nook. And Ben was there,
Humming a song upon that old black settle:
  "Or leave a kiss but in the cup
  And I'll not ask for wine."
But, meanwhile, he drank malmsey.
       Francis Bacon
Straddled before the fire; and, all at once,
He said to Shakespeare, in a voice that gripped
The Mermaid Tavern like an arctic frost:

"*There are no poets in this age of ours*
Not to compare with Plautus. They are all
Dead, the men that were famous in old days."
"Why—so they are," said Will.   The humming
    stopped.

E. MacKinstry

I saw poor Spenser, a shy gentle soul,
With haunted eyes like starlit forest pools,
Smuggling his cantos under his cloak again.
"There's verse enough, no doubt," Bacon went on,
"But English is no language for the Muse.

Whom would you call our best? There's Gabriel
    Harvey,
And Edward, Earl of Oxford. Then there's Dyer,
And Doctor Golding; while, for tragedy,
Thomas, Lord Buckhurst, hath a lofty vein.
And, in a lighter prettier vein, why, Will,
There is *thyself!* But—where's Euripides?"

"Dead," echoed Ben, in a deep ghost-like voice.
And drip—drip—drip—outside we heard the rain
Miserably dropping round the Mermaid Inn.

"Thy Summer's Night — eh, Will? Midsummer's
    Night?—
That's a quaint fancy," Bacon droned anew,
"But—Athens was an error, Will! Not Athens!
Titania knew not Athens! Those wild elves
Of thy Midsummer's Dream — eh? Midnight's
    Dream?—
Are English all. Thy woods, too, smack of England;
They never grew round Athens. Bottom, too,
He is not Greek!"
                "Greek?" Will said, with a chuckle,
"Bottom a Greek? Why, no, he was the son
Of Marian Hacket, the fat wife that kept
An ale-house, Wincot-way. I lodged with her
Walking from Stratford. You have never tramped
Along that countryside? By Burton Heath?
Ah, well, you would not know my fairylands.
It warms my blood to let my home-spuns play
Around your cold white Athens. There's a joy
In jumping time and space."
89

But, as he took
The cup of sack I proffered, solemnly
The lawyer shook his head. "Will, couldst thou use
Thy talents with discretion, and obey
Classic examples, those mightst match old Plautus,
In all except priority of the tongue.
This English tongue is only for an age,
But Latin for all time. So I propose
To embalm in Latin my philosophies.
Well seize your hour! But ere you die, you'll sail
A British galleon to the golden courts
Of Cleopatra."

"Sail it!" Marlowe roared,
Mimicking in a fit of thunderous glee
The drums and trumpets of his Tamburlaine:
"And let her buccaneers bestride the sphinx,
And play at bowls with Pharaoh's pyramids,
And hale white Egypt with their tarry hands
Home to the Mermaid! Lift the good old song
That Rob Greene loved. Gods, how the lad would
shout it!
Stand up and sing, John Davis!"

"Up!" called Raleigh,
"Lift the chanty of Black Bill's Honey-moon,
Jack!
We'll keep the chorus going!"

"Silence all!"
Ben Jonson echoed, rolling on his bench:
"This gentle lawyer hath a longing, lads,
To hear a right Homeric hymn. Now, Jack!
But wet your whistle, first! A cup of sack
For the first canto! Muscadel, the next!
Canary for the last!" I brought the cup.

John Davis emptied it at one mighty draught,
Leapt on a table, stamped with either foot,
And straight began to troll this mad sea-tale:

CANTO THE FIRST

Let Martin Parker at hawthorn-tide
  Prattle in Devonshire lanes,
Let all his pedlar poets beside
  Rattle their gallows-chains,
A tale like mine they never shall tell
  Or a merrier ballad sing,
Till the Man in the Moon pipe up the tune
  And the stars play Kiss-in-the-Ring!
Chorus: Till Philip of Spain in England reign,
        And the stars play Kiss-in-the-Ring!

All in the gorgeous dawn of day
  From grey old Plymouth Sound

Our galleon crashed thro' the crimson spray
   To sail the world around:
Cloud i' the Sun was her white-scrolled name,—
   There was never a lovelier lass
For sailing in state after pieces of eight
   With her bombards all of brass.
Chorus: Culverins, robinets, iron may-be;
           But her bombards all of brass!

Now, they that go down to the sea in ships,
   Though piracy be their trade,
For all that they pray not much with their lips
   They know where the storms are made:
With the stars above and the sharks below,
   They need not parson or clerk;
But our bo'sun Bill was an atheist still,
   Except—sometimes—in the dark!

IN THE DARK

Chorus: Now let Kit Marlowe mark!
            Our bo'sun Bill was an atheist still,
                Except—sometimes—in the dark!

All we adventured for, who shall say,
    Nor yet what our port might be?—
A magical city of old Cathay,
    Or a castle of Muscovy,
With our atheist bo'sun, Bill, Black Bill,
    Under the swinging Bear,
Whistling at night for a seaman to light
    His little poop-lanthorns there.
Chorus: On the deep, in the night, for a seaman
                to light
            His little lost lanthorns there.

But, as over the Ocean-sea we swept,
    We chanced on a strange new land
Where a valley of tall white lilies slept
    With a forest on either hand;
A valley of white in a purple wood
    And, behind it, faint and far,
Breathless and bright o'er the last rich height
    Floated the sunset-star.
Chorus: Fair and bright o'er the rose-red height,
            Venus, the sunset-star.

'Twas a marvel to see, as we beached our boat,
    Black Bill, in that peach-bloom air,
With the great white lilies that reached to his
                throat
Like a stained-glass bo'sun there,

And our little ship's chaplain, puffing and red,
  A-starn as we onward stole,
With the disk of a lily behind his head
  Like a cherubin's aureole.
Chorus: He was round and red and behind his
        head
         He'd a cherubin's aureole.

"Hyrcania, land of honey and bees,
  We have found thee at last," he said,
"Where the honey-comb swells in the hollow
    trees."
  (O, the lily behind his head!)
"The honey-comb swells in the purple wood!
  'Tis the swette which the heavens distil,
Saith Pliny himself, on my little book-shelf!
  Is the world not sweet to thee, Bill?"
Chorus: "Saith Pliny himself, on my little book-
      shelf!
        Is the world not sweet to thee, Bill?"

Now a man may taste of the devil's hot spice,
  And yet if his mind run back
To the honey of childhood's Paradise
  His heart is not wholly black;
And Bill, Black Bill, from the days of his youth
  Tho' his chest was broad as an oak,
Had cherished one innocent little sweet tooth,
  And it itched as our chaplain spoke.
Chorus: He had kept one perilous little tooth,
        And it itched as our chaplain spoke.

All around was a mutter of bees,
  And Bill 'gan muttering too,—
"If the honey-comb swells in the hollow trees,
  (What else can a Didymus do?)
I'll steer to the purple woods myself
  And see if this thing be so,
Which the chaplain found on his little book-shelf,
  For Pliny lived long ago."
Chorus: There's a platter of delf on his little
            book-shelf,
          And Pliny lived long ago.

Scarce had he spoken when, out of the wood,
  And buffeting all around,
Rooting our sea-boots where we stood,
  There rumbled a marvellous sound,
As a mountain of honey were crumbling
            asunder,
  Or a sunset-avalanche hurled
Honey-comb boulders of golden thunder
  To smother the old black world.
Chorus: Honey-comb boulders of musical
            thunder
          To mellow this old black world.

And the chaplain he whispered — "This honey,
            one saith,
  On my camphired cabin-shelf,
None may harvest on pain of death;
  For the bee would eat it himself!
None walketh those woods but him whose voice
  In the dingles you then did hear!"

"A Voice?" growls Bill. "Ay, Bill, r-r-rejoice!
   'Twas the great Hyrcanian Bear!"
Chorus: Give thanks! *Re*-joice! 'Twas the
         glor-r-r-ious Voice
      Of the great Hyrcanian Bear!

But, marking that Bill looked bitter indeed,
   For his sweet tooth hungered sore,
"Consider," he saith, "that the Sweet hath need
   Of the Sour, as the Sea of the Shore!
As the night to the day is our grief to our joy,
   And each for its brother prepares
A banquet, Bill, that would otherwise cloy,
   Thus is it with honey and bears."
Chorus: Roses and honey and laughter would
         cloy!
      Give us thorns, too, and sorrow and
         bears!

"Consider," he saith, "how by fretting a string
   The lutanist maketh sweet moan,
And a bird ere it fly must have air for its wing
   To buffet or fall like a stone:
Tho' you blacken like Pluto you make but more
         white
   These blooms which not Enna could yield!
Consider, Black Bill, ere the coming of night,
   The lilies," he saith, "of the field."
Chorus: "Consider, Black Bill, in this beautiful
         light,
      The lilies," he saith, "of the field."

"Consider the claws of a Bear," said Bill,
   "That can rip off the flesh from your bones,
While his belly could cabin the skipper and still
   Accommodate Timothy Jones!
Why, that's where a seaman who cares for his
      grog
   Perspires how this world isn't square!
If there's *cause* for a *cow*, if there's *use* for a *dog*,
   By Pope John, there's no *Sense* in a *Bear!*"
Chorus: Cause for a cow, use for a dog,
         By'r Lakin, no *Sense* in a *Bear!*

But our little ship's chaplain—"Sense," quoth he,
   "Hath the Bear tho' his making have none;
For, my little book saith, by the sting of this bee
   Would Ursus be wholly foredone,

But, or ever the hive he adventureth nigh
  And its crisp gold-crusted dome,
He lardeth his nose and he greaseth his eye
  With a piece of an honey-comb."
Chorus: His velvety nose and his sensitive eye
    With a piece of an honey-comb.

Black Bill at the word of that golden crust
  —For his ears had forgotten the roar,
And his eyes grew soft with their innocent lust—
  'Gan licking his lips once more:
"Be it bound like a missal and printed as fair,
  With capitals blue and red,
'Tis a lie; for what honey could comfort a bear,
  Till the bear win the honey?" he said.
Chorus: "Ay, *whence* the first honey wherewith
      the first bear
    First larded his nose?" he said.

"Thou first metaphysical bo'sun, Bill,"
  Our chaplain quizzingly cried,
"Wilt thou riddle me redes of a dumpling still
  With thy 'how came the apple inside?' "
"Nay," answered Bill, "but I quest for truth,
  And I find it not on your shelf!
I will face your Hyrcanian bear, forsooth,
  And look at his nose myself."
Chorus: For truth, for truth, or a little sweet
      tooth—
    I will into the woods myself.

Breast-high thro' that foam-white ocean of
    bloom
   With its wonderful spokes of gold,
Our sun-burnt crew in the rose-red gloom
   Like buccaneer galleons rolled:
Breast-high, breast-high in the lilies we stood,
   And before we could say "good-night,"
Out of the valley and into the wood
   He plunged thro' the last rich light.
Chorus: Out of the lilies and into the wood,
       Where the Great Bear walks all
       night!

And our little ship's chaplain he piped thro' the
    trees
  As the moon rose, white and still,
"Hylas, return to thy Heracles!"
  And we helped him with "Come back, Bill!"
Thrice he piped it, thrice we halloo'd,
  And thrice we were dumb to hark;
But never an answer came from the wood,
  So—we turned to our ship in the dark.
Chorus: Good-bye, Bill! you're a Didymus still;
         But—you're all alone in the dark.

"This honey now"—as the first canto ceased,
The great young Bacon pompously began—
"Which Pliny calleth, as it were, the swette
Of heaven, or spettle of the stars, is found
In Muscovy. Now . . ." "Bring the muscadel,"
Ben Johnson roared—" 'Tis a more purple drink,
And suits with the next canto!"
                                        At one draught
John Davis drained the cup, and with one hand
Beating the measure, rapidly trolled again.

102

CANTO THE SECOND

Now, Rabelais, art thou quite foredone,
Dan Chaucer, Drayton, Every One!
Leave we aboard our *Cloud i' the Sun*
    This crew of pirates dreaming—
Of Angels, minted in the blue
Like golden moons, Rose-nobles, too,
As under the silver-sliding dew
    Our emerald creek lay gleaming!
Chorus: Under the stars lay gleaming!

And mailed with scales of gold and green
The high star-lilied banks between,
Nosing our old black hulk unseen,
    Great alligators shimmered:
Blood-red jaws i' the blue-black ooze,
Where all the long warm day they snooze,
Chewing old cuds of pirate-crews,
    Around us grimly glimmered.
Chorus: Their eyes like rubies glimmered.

Let us now sing of Bill, good sirs!
Follow him, all green forestéres,
Fearless of Hyrcanian bears
    As of these ghostly lilies!
For O, not Drayton there could sing
Of wild Pigwiggen and his King
So merry a jest, so jolly a thing
    As this my tale of Bill is.
Chorus: Into the woods where Bill is!

Now starts he as a white owl hoots,
And now he stumbles over roots,
And now beneath his big sea-boots
   In yon deep glade he crunches
Black cakes of honey-comb that were
So elfin-sweet, perchance, last year;
But neither Bo'sun, now, nor Bear
   At that dark banquet munches.
Chorus: Onward still he crunches!

Black cakes of honey-comb he sees
Above him in the forks of trees,
Filled by stars instead of bees,
   With brimming silver glisten:
But ah, such food of gnome and fay
Could neither Bear nor Bill delay
Till where yon ferns and moonbeams play
   He starts and stands to listen!
Chorus: What melody doth he listen?

Is it the Night-Wind as it comes
Through the wood and softly thrums
Silvery tabors, purple drums,
   To speed some wild-wood revel?
Nay, Didymus, what faint sweet din
Of viol and flute and violin
Makes all the forest round thee spin,
   The Night-Wind or the Devil?
Chorus: No doubt at all—the Devil!

He stares, with naked knife in hand,
This buccaneer in fairyland!
Dancing in a saraband
  The red ferns reel about him!
Dancing in a morrice-ring
The green ferns curtsey, kiss and cling!
Their Marians flirt, their Robins fling
  Their feathery heels to flout him!
Chorus: The whole wood reels about him.

Dance, ye shadows! O'er the glade,
Bill, the Bo'sun, undismayed,
Pigeon-toes with glittering blade!
    Drake was never bolder!
Devil or Spaniard, what cares he
Whence your eerie music be?
Till—lo, against yon old oak-tree
    He leans his brawny shoulder!
Chorus: He lists and leans his shoulder!

Ah, what melody doth he hear
As to that gnarled old tree-trunk there
He lays his wind-bit brass-ringed ear,
    And steals his arm about it?
What Dryad could this Bo'sun win
To that slow-rippling amorous grin?—
'Twas full of singing bees within!
    Not Didymus could doubt it!
Chorus: So loud they buzzed about it!

Straight, o'er a bough one leg he throws,
And up that oaken main-mast goes
With reckless red unlarded nose
    And gooseberry eyes of wonder!
Till now, as in a galleon's hold,
Below, he sees great cells of gold
Whence all the hollow trunk up-rolled
    A low melodious thunder.
Chorus: A sweet and perilous thunder!

Ay, there, within that hollow tree,
Will Shakespeare, mightst thou truly see
The Imperial City of the Bee,
  In Chrysomelan splendour!
And, in the midst, one eight-foot dome
Swells o'er that Titan honey-comb
Where the Bee-Empress hath her home,
  With such as do attend her.
Chorus: Weaponed with stings attend her!

But now her singing sentinels
Have turned to sleep in waxen cells,
And Bill leans down his face and smells
    The whole sweet summer's cargo—
In one deep breath, the whole year's bloom,
Lily and thyme and rose and broom,
One Golden Fleece of flower-perfume
    In that old oaken Argo.
Chorus: That green and golden Argo!

And now he hangs with dangling feet
Over that dark abyss of sweet,
Striving to reach such wild gold meat
    As none could buy for money:
His left hand grips a swinging branch
When—crack! Our Bo'sun, stout and stanch,
Falls like an Alpine avalanche,
    Feet first into the honey!
Chorus: Up to his ears in honey!

And now his red unlarded nose
And bulging eyes are all that shows
Above it, as he puffs and blows!
    And now—to 'scape the scathing
Of that black host of furious bees
His nose and eyes he fain would grease
And bobs below those golden seas
    Like an old woman bathing.
Chorus: Old Mother Hubbard bathing!

And now he struggles, all in vain,
To reach some little bough again;
But, though he heaves with might and main,
  This honey holds his ribs, sirs,
So tight, a barque might sooner try
To steer a cargo through the sky
Than Bill, thus honey-logged, to fly
  By flopping of his jib, sirs!
Chorus: His tops'l and his jib, sirs!

Like Oberon in the hive his beard
With wax and honey all besmeared
Would make the crescent moon afeard
  That now is sailing brightly
Right o'er his leafy donjon-keep!
But that she knows him sunken deep,
And that his tower is straight and steep,
  She would not smile so lightly.
Chorus: Look down and smile so lightly.

She smiles in that small heavenly space,
Ringed with the tree-trunk's leafy grace,
While upward grins his ghastly face
  As if some wild-wood Satyr,
Some gnomish Ptolemy should dare
Up that dark optic tube to stare,
As all unveiled she floated there,
  Poor maiden moon, straight at her!
Chorus: The buccaneering Satyr!

But there, till some one help him out,
Black Bill must stay, without a doubt,
"Help! Help!" he gives a muffled shout!
      None but the white owls hear it!
Who? Whoo? they cry: Bill answers "Me!
I am stuck fast in this great tree!
Bring me a rope, good Timothy!
      There's honey, lads, we'll share it!"
Chorus: Ay, now he wants to share it.

Then, thinking help may come with morn,
He sinks, half-famished and out-worn,
And scarce his nose exalts its horn
      Above that sea of glory!
But, even as he owns defeat,
His belly saith, "A man must eat,
And since there is none other meat,
      Come, lap this mess before 'ee!"
Chorus: This glorious mess before 'ee.

Then Dian sees a right strange sight
As, bidding him a fond good-night,
She flings a silvery kiss to light
      In that deep oak-tree hollow,
And finds that gold and crimson nose
A moving, munching, ravenous rose
That up and down unceasing goes,
      Save when he stops to swallow!
Chorus: He finds it hard to swallow!

Ay, now his best becomes his worst,
For honey cannot quench his thirst,
Though he should eat until he burst;
　　But, ah, the skies are kindly,
And from their tender depths of blue
They send their silver-sliding dew.
So Bill thrusts out his tongue anew
　　And waits to catch it—blindly!
Chorus: For ah, the stars are kindly!

And sometimes, with a shower of rain,
They strive to ease their prisoner's pain:
Then Bill thrusts out his tongue again
　　With never a grace, the sinner!
And day and night and day goes by,
And never a comrade comes anigh,
And still the honey swells as high
　　For supper, breakfast, dinner!
Chorus: Yet Bill has grown no thinner!

The young moon grows to full and throws
Her buxom kiss upon his nose,
As nightly over the tree she goes,
　　And peeps and smiles and passes,
Then with her fickle silver flecks
Our old black galleon's dreaming decks;
And then her face, with nods and becks,
　　In midmost ocean glasses.
Chorus: 'Twas ever the way with lasses!

Ah, Didymus, hast thou won indeed
That Paradise which is thy meed?
(Thy tale not all that run may read!)
    Thy sweet hath now no leaven!
Now, like an onion in a cup
Of mead, thou liest for Jove to sup,
Could Polyphemus lift thee up
    With Titan hands to heaven!
Chorus: This great oak-cup to heaven!

The second canto ceased; and, as they raised
Their wine-cups with the last triumphant note,
Bacon, undaunted, raised his grating voice—
"This honey which, in some sort, may be styled
The Spettle of the Stars . . ." "Bring the Canary!"
Ben Jonson roared. "It is a moral wine
And suits the third, last canto!" At one draught
John Davis drained it and began anew.

A month went by. We were hoisting sail!
  We had lost all hope of Bill;
Though, laugh as you may at a seaman's tale,
  He was fast in his honey-comb still!
And often he thinks of the chaplain's word
  In the days he shall see no more,—
How the Sweet, indeed, of the Sour hath need;
  And the Sea, likewise, of the Shore.
Chorus: The chaplain's word of the Air and a
        Bird;
        Of the Sea, likewise, and the Shore!

"O, had I the wings of a dove, I would fly
  To a heaven, of aloes and gall!
I have honeyed," he yammers, "my nose and mine
      eye,
  And the bees cannot sting me at all!

And it's O, for the sting of a little brown bee,
   Or to blister my hands on a rope,
Or to buffet a thundering broad-side sea
   On a deck like a mountain-slope!"
Chorus: With her mast snapt short, and a list to
           port
           And a deck like a mountain-slope.

But alas, and he thinks of the chaplain's voice
   When that roar from the woods out-break—
R-r-re-joice! R-r-re-joice! "Now, wherefore
      rejoice
   In the music a bear could make?

'Tis a judgment, maybe, that I stick in this tree;
    Yet in this I out-argued him fair!
Though I live, though I die, in this honey-comb
    pie,
    By Pope Joan, there's no sense in a bear!"
Chorus: Notes in a nightingale, plums in a pie,
        By'r Lakin, no *Sense* in a *Bear!*

He knew not our anchor was heaved from the
    mud:
    He was growling it over again,
When—a strange sound suddenly froze his blood,
    And curdled his big slow brain!—
A marvellous sound, as of great steel claws
    Gripping the bark of his tree,
Softly ascended! Like lightning ended
    His honey-comb reverie!
Chorus: The honey-comb quivered! The little
        leaves shivered!
        Something was climbing the tree!

Something that breathed like a fat sea-cook,
    Or a pirate of fourteen ton!
But it clomb like a cat (tho' the whole tree shook)
    Stealthily tow'rds the sun,

Till, as Black Bill gapes at the little blue ring
  Overhead, which he calls the sky,
It is clean blotted out by a monstrous Thing
  Which—*hath larded its nose and its eye.*
Chorus: O, well for thee, Bill, that this
              monstrous Thing
          Hath blinkered its little red eye.

Still as a mouse lies Bill with his face
  Low down in the dark sweet gold,
While this monster turns round in the leaf-
              fringed space!
  Then—taking a good firm hold,
As the skipper descending the cabin-stair,
  Tail-first with a vast slow tread,
Solemnly, softly, cometh this Bear
  Straight down o'er the Bo'sun's head.
Chorus: Solemnly—slowly—cometh this Bear,
          Tail-first, o'er the Bo'sun's head.

Nearer—nearer—then all Bill's breath
  Out-bursts in one leap and yell!
And this Bear thinks, "Now am I gripped from
              beneath
  By a roaring devil from hell!"
And madly Bill clutches his brown bow-legs,
  And madly this Bear doth hale,
With his little red eyes fear-mad for the skies
  And Bill's teeth fast in his tail!

117

Chorus: Small wonder a Bear should quail!
To have larded his nose, to have greased
his eyes,
And be stung at the last in his tail.

Pull, Bo'sun! Pull, Bear! In the hot sweet gloom,
Pull Bruin, pull Bill, for the skies!
Pull—out of their gold with a bombard's boom
Come Black Bill's honeyed thighs!
Pull! Up! Up! Up! with a scuffle and scramble,
To that little blue ring of bliss,
This Bear doth go with our Bo'sun in tow
Stinging his tail, I wis.
Chorus: And this Bear thinks—"Many great
bees I know,
But there never was Bee like this!"

.   .   .   .

All in the gorgeous death of day
We had slipped from our emerald creek,
And our *Cloud i' the Sun* was careening away
With the old gay flag at the peak,
When, suddenly, out of the purple wood,
Breast-high thro' the lilies there danced
A tall lean figure, black as a nigger,
That shouted and waved and pranced!
Chorus: A gold-greased figure, but black as a
nigger,
Waving his shirt as he pranced!

118

Pull, Bo'sun! Pull, Bear!

119

" 'Tis Hylas! 'Tis Hylas!" our chaplain flutes,
    And our skipper he looses a shout!
" 'Tis Bill! Black Bill, in his old sea-boots!
    Stand by to bring her about!
Har-r-rd a-starboard!" And round we came,
    With a lurch and a dip and a roll,
And a banging boom thro' the rose-red gloom
    For our old Black Bo'sun's soul!
Chorus: Alive! Not dead! Tho' behind his head
          He'd a seraphin's aureole!

    •   •   •   •   •   •   •

And our chaplain he sniffs, as Bill finished his tale,
(With the honey still scenting his hair!)

O'er a plate of salt beef and a mug of old ale—
 "By Pope Joan, there's no sense in a bear!"
And we laughed, but our Bo'sun he solemnly
            growls
    —"Till the sails of yon heavens be furled,
It taketh — now, mark! — all the beasts in the
        Ark,
    Teeth and claws, too, to make a good world!"

Chorus: Till the great—blue—sails—be—
                furled,
            It taketh—now, mark!—all the beasts
            in the Ark,
                Teeth and claws, too, to make a good
                world!

E. MacKinstry

"Sack! Sack! Canary! Malmsey! Muscadel!"—
As the last canto ceased, the Mermaid Inn
Chorussed. I flew from laughing voice to voice;
But, over all the hubbub, rose the drone
Of Francis Bacon,—"Now, this Muscovy
Is a cold clime, not favorable to bees
(Or love, which is a weakness of the south)
As well might be supposed. Yet, as hot lands
Gender hot fruits and odoriferous spice,
In this case we may think that honey and flowers
Are comparable with the light airs of May
And a more temperate region. Also we see,
As Pliny saith, this honey being a swette
Of heaven, a certain spettle of the stars,
Which, gathering unclean vapours as it falls,
Hangs as a fat dew on the boughs, the bees
Obtain it partly thus, and afterwards
Corrupt it in their stomachs, and at last
123

Expel it through their mouths and harvest it
In hives; yet, of its heavenly source it keeps
A great part. Thus, by various principles
Of natural philosophy we observe—"
And, as he leaned to Drayton, droning thus,
I saw a light gleam of celestial mirth
Flit o'er the face of Shakespeare—scarce a smile—
A swift irradiation from within
As of a cloud that softly veils the sun.